100 Years of UPHILL CASTLE CRICKET CLUB

by
Richard Twort

Printed by
Tasker Printers Ltd
Lynx Crescent, Weston-super-Mare

Published by
The Uphill Struggle Marketing Company
7, South Road, Weston-super-Mare

ISBN 0 9520680 0 1

CONTENTS

Department of National Heritage 5
Foreword - Lt. Col. C.D.C. Frith OBE, President 6
PREFACE 8
INTRODUCTION 11
The Chairman - Graham Board 12
The Early Years 1893 - 1920 15
The 1920's 21
The 1930's 27
The 1940's 35
The 1950's 45
The 1960's 53
The 1970's 61
The 1980's 67
The 1990's 75
Somerset County Cricket Club 94
The Future 95
Club Officers 96
The Test and County Cricket Board 99
Acknowledgments 100

DEPARTMENT OF NATIONAL HERITAGE
Horse Guards Road, London SW1P 3AL
Telephone 071-270 5791
Facsimile 071-270 6026

From the Under Secretary of State
ROBERT KEY MP

I am delighted to provide this message of support to mark the centenary of Uphill Castle Cricket Club.

Local clubs such as yours form the foundations of cricket in this country and give members of the local community the chance to participate. The future of the club is also important and by encouraging younger members to join and improve their skills, you are assuring both your continued success and the health of cricket in general.

100 years of cricket at the club must have seen many important milestones and you must all share many happy memories of past achievements. With the cricket season under way again, I hope this special year will prove more successful than ever and will set you on the road to your bicentenary.

Robert Key

ROBERT KEY

FOREWORD

Lt.Col C.D.C. Frith, O.B.E.

A centenary is a noteworthy achievement, so it is most fitting that it should be marked by the production of a history of the Club. We owe Richard Twort a considerable debt of gratitude for taking on the task.

Uphill Castle from which the Club takes its name, only became Uphill Manor because my Grandmother, Edith Graves-Knyfton, refused to live in a Castle! So far as I can discover the house was built in 1805 by one Simon Payne who married the daughter and heiress of the Rev. Jonathan Gegg who built and lived in Uphill House (now Uphill Grange). Payne was imprisoned for debt and the property was bought by the Rev. John Henry Gegg who ran a school there. He lost all his money and in 1825 went to Jamaica, returning later to live at Sunnyside, Moorland Road until his death in 1911 aged 93. In 1830 Uphill Castle passed to a relation of Simon Payne, Daniel Beaumont Payne. It took him only two years to be declared bankrupt and the property was bought at auction in 1832 by Thomas Tutton Knyfton (the second - his father was also Thomas Tutton Knyfton!). He died without surviving issue and the entailed estate passed to his nephew, my grandfather, Reginald Benett Graves, who complied with the provisions of the will by taking the name Knyfton. He died in India in 1918 after being badly wounded in Mesopotamia.

He had been closely associated with the Club from its inception and after his death his elder daughter, Marjorie, became President and remained so for a record 73 years. I have always taken an interest (a trifle sporadic perhaps, because of my prolonged absences from Uphill!) in the Club and could have been seen from time to time peering over the hedge to watch matches in progress, so was delighted and honoured to be asked to continue the family association by accepting the position of President. I played for the Club occasionally in my later years at school during the time when Joe Cossens was Chairman. The fact that I cannot recollect anything about my achievements perhaps bears out the suggestion that things best forgotten are most easily forgotten!

I trust that Richard's history and my Presidency will together launch Uphill Castle Cricket Club on a second successful century, played out on the same attractive field as the first.

Colin Frith *October 1992*

PREFACE

Richard Twort

I am indebted to the many players, past and present, who have helped in supplying me with material for this publication. After suggesting to my committee that we produce such a book to celebrate our centenary, I got the distinct impression that all eyes were on me when it came to volunteers. It was only after the initial euphoria had died down that I realised what a daunting task this was to be and I have to say that without continuous encouragement from all quarters, the book would still be in it's embryo stage at the 125th anniversary!

When I joined Uphill Castle with my old friend Bob Davies more than 20 years ago, I clearly recall him saying that my bank manager was a cricket fan and he would really appreciate reading the match reports of my heroic exploits and therefore ensure that I would be held in much higher esteem. Dear old Bob - always full of useful theories. Even if this one were true I never really found out because 'heroic exploits', particularly on the cricket field, were never my strong point.

On my arrival at the club, and rather in awe of the legendary Jack Bickell, I said I would be happy to play in the seconds but only if they were short. I was duly selected but on Friday evening Jack saw me arrive at the ground and said "is that your car"? I confirmed it was and he instantly promoted me to the firsts as their Saturday fixture was an away game. Strangely enough most of my games that year were away!

Other cherished memories of Uphill are watching Frank O'Brien demolish the tool shed at his first attempt on the motor mower; falling out of a tree whilst whiling away the hours at deep third man; of Martyn Edwards doing the fandango after standing on a wasps nest; going out to bat at 2.0 o'clock in the morning; Doc Holyday's ton; helping Roy Curry up to his knees in water trying to prepare a wicket; Roger Fry's huge notice deep in a fenced off area of scrub and brambles where no one has ever been, advertising 'Keep out - Very Rare Flowers'. The notorious 'wig' incident; Somerset's Graham Burgess getting out first ball in his benefit match and explosive centuries from Len Beale, Huw Jenkins and Gareth Williams.

I could go on and on but these pages are far too precious for my personal recollections and ramblings. There are articles and photographs on previous decades, contributed by past and present players, together with features and stories which I hope will offer a wider appeal to cricket lovers everywhere. This book is intended not only as a partial historic guide to Uphill Castle Cricket Club, but also as a tribute to the game itself. As a humble writer (and even humbler cricketer), I hope I have gone some way in achieving these objectives.

Richard Twort

*Have you not ever felt the urge to write of
all the cricket that has blessed your sight?*

*Is there no inspiration in the names of
those that play the best of summer games?*

INTRODUCTION

It's 24th June 1992, a gloriously sunny and warm Midsummer's day. As I sit in our little wooden pavilion penning this introduction whilst waiting my turn at the crease my thoughts drift back and I wonder what it would have been like back in the 1890's. The world news of the day would be about the fighting between Japan and China, clashes in Egypt, the Boer war and numerous other such conflicts. But I suppose little of that would have mattered to Uphill Castle and their opponents way back in the heyday of the Victorian era.

How little would they have thought about the cares of the world whilst striding out to bat for the honour of the village against the traditional fast bowling blacksmith from the neighbouring hamlet.

I hope they thought even less of the future for many would come to die on a foreign field in a country they new little about for a cause even more remote. Indeed this 'War of all wars' coincided with Uphill's 25th Anniversary as did the 50th (the Jubilee) conflict with World War 2. One wonders if Uphill pessimists feared their 75th anniversary celebrations would be impaired by yet another global conflict this time emanating from Vietnam.

Enough of these morbid reflections, this is a time of celebration! We've made it! We are 100 years old. Crash! Another wicket falls and I must away to the crease. As I stride forth do I think of the crisis in Yugoslavia, the Gulf War, the worst recession in the history of the Modern World - do these matters affect me? of course they do - just look at my appalling batting average!

Slug

Chairman - General Allrounder

Graham Board

I thought it appropriate to have a heading linked with this game we love. I also believe it appropriate that the heading sums-up the tasks that a working Chairman has to fulfil with an amateur sports club.

Looking back at my first year as Chairman, I really do feel a sense of success, as my main objective when I took over the position was to get more people involved and I believe that this, with the help of the others, has been achieved.

1992 was full of action on and off the field, staring way back in January with our skittles evening at the Rugby Club, then onto February, when a number of us participated in a 'pub treasure hunt', an evening enjoyed by everyone. March saw a group of us visit Lord's, a day I won't forget, not every club cricketer has the opportunity to walk through the Long room, have a guided tour of the ground and then use the indoor nets, where most of the "cricketing greats" have practised. April had the 'club' cavorting the night away in barn dance style, which also turned to be our most lucrative fund-raiser of the year ... a brilliant night! The summer months of course actually saw us get round to playing cricket with a packed season - 4 Saturday league sides, one Sunday, one midweek evening, one midweek plus the touring side (under some superb organisation, the club toured Yorkshire for a second time), all played in the true spirit of the game.

During September, we held our annual dinner and dance, where club presentations were made to (congratulations again) Dave Bickell, for player of the year, Dave Thorne, young player of the year, Mike Holyday, for his maiden century and for Clubman of the year and Jack Rowan, who was awarded the 'Special Award' for his services to the club, bearing in mind for the last six seasons he has travelled half-way round the world to play for Uphill.

October, we sorted the ground out for winter and finally in November, a 'Race Night' is organised - unfortunately, this has been written before the evening, so I can't publish the results ...but hopefully another profitable evening!

Finally, I could list a great number of people to thank, but they know who they are, all I would like to say is ... let's do it again, during 1993 - and to wish you all an enjoyable centenary season.

Graham Board
Chairman

Who but an Englishman would understand the significance of Beatty, while pursuing the marauding Dervishes up the Nile in December 1897, when he recorded in his diary between skirmishes.......

"the cricket kit has arrived".

THE EARLY YEARS
1893 - 1920

Uphill Castle Cricket Club has been inextricably linked with the Graves-Knyfton family ever since its first tenuous steps in 1893.

It was a great social occasion when the family took up residence in the Uphill Manor a year earlier in 1892 and they celebrated their arrival by inviting the whole village including 150 children to a tea and concert at the Castle. The Gazette of the 11th June 1892 recalls: "The children were conducted to the front terrace where they sang several school songs in the presence of Mrs Graves and family together with a party of visitors. The songs selected gave great satisfaction and Mrs Graves complimented the scholars upon the quality and sweetness of tone which characterised their singing". In the evening a concert was held which the Gazette described: "as a brilliant success, and one of the finest exhibitions of musical talent ever witnessed at Uphill".

Major R. B. Graves-Knyfton
President 1893 - 1918

Miss E. M. Graves-Knyfton
President 1919 - 1992

Until 1893, cricket at Uphill was played by a team known as the Boulevard Club and coincidentally, was made up mainly of the male staff of Uphill Manor. However, on June 5th 1893 some local village stalwarts put their heads together and decided to form a cricket club which would really be properly representative of the whole village. It would be called Uphill Castle Cricket Club.

The manor put its full support behind the idea and actually paid for each mans full set of kit including his club tie, an article without which a cricketer of that era was not considered properly dressed.

A Cricket ground had been prepared in front of the Castle called the Manor Field and for a short time this became the home of Uphill Castle cricket club. Although early matches were recorded as "successful" the very first game, an away fixture at Mark was a disaster, as the Castle were dismissed for 4 runs and two of those were byes.

For reasons lost in the mists of time Uphill Castle moved after a few years to St John's Playing Fields (then called Fifty Acres) and later still moving to a ground known as Hocker's Field where Stanhope Road and Totterdown Road are now situated.

A sombre report in the 1st May 1915 Edition of the Mercury states that at the annual meeting, Mr A Hobbs suggested that the club should disband for the season on account of the war. Although the club had arranged a few fixtures, these were mostly against schools. Mr Hobbs observed that it was a question of finding time to play and personally he did not desire to continue under the circumstances. Mr Parker thought that if the officers were not elected the club might disappear altogether.

After what appears to have been a lengthy meeting, it was agreed to continue the club and Major Reginald Graves-Knyfton was re-elected as president with Col. Whitting, Captain Sandys and Mr B H Hill being Vice Presidents. The club captain was Mr Morgan Whitting. Old local names such as Hicks, Masters, Williams, Minife and Clarke were also elected to the committee. George Masters was in fact the clubs first Hon. Secretary,

The luxury of the motor car or coach was not available in the early years, so the horse drawn wagonette, and the bicycle were used to travel to away games. Sometimes even the railway carried the team because Uphill Station, pictured here, was fully operational in those days.

The oldest surviving team photograph - 1901

treasurer and general factotum and was to look after the clubs interest for more than forty years.

With the Great War finally behind them, a meeting was held on May 1st 1919 at the village school to consider restarting cricket which had been suspended like all other similar clubs (except public schools).

The Chairman, Mr B. H. Hill, now a J.P. paid a warm tribute to the late President, Major Graves-Knyfton, who had suffered war wounds in Mesopotamia and later died at a remote out-station in Southern India. He had been President for the whole of the club's life and had always taken a very keen interest in it's welfare.

His daughter, Miss Edith Marjorie Graves-Knyfton was unanimously elected President of the club, a post she was to hold for an astonishing seventy three years until her death in September 1992.

Cricket eventually got underway towards the end of May with a match between the married men and single men. History does not record the result, but more serious cricket started the following week with an away match against Worle which the Castle lost by 29 runs. However matters improved considerably after this, in fact they never lost another match during the 1919 season, beating teams like Brent Knoll (three times!), Weston A and Weston 2nds, Highbridge, Hunstpill and district and Banwell. The latter being dismissed for a mere 9 on the 13th September. Banwell were obviously keen to avenge this embarrassment but were quickly bowled out for 22 the following week!. The Castle also turned the tables on Worle, beating them at the home ground by 98 runs. At the end of this particular match both teams were entertained to tea at the manor by Mrs & Miss Graves-Knyfton.

Uphill Castle Cricket Club obviously ended the decade on a high note and looked forward to thrilling encounters in the new era which was to follow.

Uphill Village at around the turn of the century

Uphill Manor as it was in the early 1900's - little has changed over the years. It was in the field next to the manor that cricket in Uphill started in 1893

Miss Graves-Kryfton sits proudly in front of the Uphill Team before a match in the 1920's.

THE TWENTIES

Cricket at Uphill was always played in the proper spirit and on balance the Castle won more than they lost. However it must be said that from the sparse records available it appears that the bowlers always seemed to have the upper hand as the following averages for the 1923 season will testify.

Matches played, 28: 13 won: 10 lost: 3 drawn: 2 abandoned through rain.

Batting	Inns.	N.O.	Runs.	Best	Avg.
H Hart	17	1	337	60	21.1
E Parker	19	1	235	67	13.1
R Shannon	6	0	63	25	10.5
H Marsh	16	1	157	40	10.4
H Price	14	1	129	39	9.9
C Parker	17	1	152	33	9.5
G Phillips	15	4	91	13	8.3
E Porter	13	1	63	16	5.3
S Hart	12	1	41	15	3.7
F Clark	13	3	34	10	3.4
E Williams	14	2	36	12	3.0
C Patch	15	4	20	11	1.8

Bowling	Overs	Maiden Overs	Runs	Wkts.	Avg.
H Price	115	34	212	40	5.33
E Parker	185	44	375	61	6.10
H Marsh	39	7	96	13	7.31
E Williams	88	13	232	30	7.73
C Parker	106	20	266	27	9.85

Much discussion took place at the annual general meeting that year about plans for a new pavilion - a topic which was to become very familiar over the years!

Excerpt from the Gazette - October 27th 1923

UPHILL CASTLE C.C.
Plans For The Provision Of A New Pavilion

The annual meeting of the Uphill Castle Cricket Club was held on Tuesday evening, and was well attended. The chair was occupied by that esteemed and generous friend of the Club, Mr. B.H. Hill J.P. and those present included Messrs. S.R. Feaver, R. Shannon, A.H. Hobbs, E. Williams, F. Clark, G. Langford. T. Porter, H. Hart, E. Parker, W. Popham, F.W. Shearmur, E. Adams, W. Howe, G. Phillips, S. Hart, J.M. Hart, C. Patch and G. R. Masters (hon. secretary and treasurer).

Mr. Masters produced the accounts for the past year, which showed a net balance in hand on all accounts of £12/2/10. Proceeding, the Secretary gave a detailed account of the splendid efforts the committee had made this last season in raising various sums for relaying the cricket pitch, work which cost the club £32/9/0. This was carried out by Mr. H.J. Kingdon in the most satisfactory manner.

The watch competition produced for the club a net balance of £11/3/11. The club's best thanks were due to the following ladies and gentlemen, who this season undertook the duty of providing teas on the ground for the home matches: Miss Williams and Mrs. Mann, assisted by Mr. W. Popham. The net proceeds from this venture produced a balance for the club of £2/14/0.

Mr. Hill, in moving the adoption of the accounts, remarked that the committee had made a splendid effort in raising various sums for the club since their last meeting, thereby putting the club in a good financial position. The club's thanks, he said, were due to the hon. secretary for the very able way in which he had presented these various accounts.

The resolution was seconded by Mr. F.W. Shearmur and carried with acclamation.

The election of officers was then proceeded with. On the proposition of the Chairman, Miss Graves-Knyfton was unanimously re-elected President of the Club, and last year's vice-presidents were re-elected en bloc, with the addition of Mr. F. Shearmur. Mr. E. Williams was re-elected captain and Mr. C. Parker vice-captain.

The following were elected members of the committee: Messrs, E. Williams, C. Parker, I. Hart, E. Parker, T. Porter, G. Langford, E. Adams, W. Popham, F. Clark. H. Hart, C. Minifie and R. Shannon. Mr G.R. Masters was unanimously re-elected secretary and treasurer, and on the proposition of the Chairman was heartily thanked for the valuable services he had rendered the club for so many years.

Mr. Masters in acknowledging the compliment said he would continue to carry out the duties for another year. It was a work he had very much at heart, and to him cricket was far and away beyond other national games, and if played in the right spirit was a most manly game.

Mr. Hill said there was one more item on the agenda to consider, and that was the question of a new pavilion. The old one was getting in a very bad state, having stood the storms for many years, and the committee this winter were going to make every effort to provide funds towards the provision of a new one. The Chairman remarked that as the committee were anxious to provide a new pavilion and it was really necessary to do so, he would be pleased to give a donation of £5 towards this object. Mr. S. R. Feaver also said he would be pleased to help in this matter and would promise to be responsible for £5 for this deserving object before Christmas. Needless to say cordial thanks were expressed to these gentlemen for their generosity.

A committee will be formed at an early date and the work put in hand as soon as the estimated cost has been procured.

Before closing the meeting the secretary proposed on behalf of the club a hearty vote of thanks to the following gentlemen, who had given so much time in various ways to the club: Messrs, F. Clark, G. Langford and J. Hart. On the motion of Mr. F. Shearmur, a hearty vote of thanks was accorded the Chairman for presiding. Mr. Hill, in reply, said it would be a real pleasure at all times to do everything in his power for the Uphill Castle C.C.

Mr. Williams announced that Messrs, M. Whitting and Mr. R.A. Riddell had kindly offered to give prizes for the best bowling and batting averages. This concluded what was probably the most successful meeting in the club's history. The annual dinner is fixed for Nov. 22.

This photograph taken in the early 1920's shows Mr Howe's Rooms (to the right of the Dolphin) where the club held their annual dinners for many years. These rooms were also known as Crooks Tea Rooms - so called because when the builders were completing the building and putting the finishing touches to the chimney stack, they could just make out the top of Crooks Peak in the distance.

The Annual Dinner

This early 20's annual dinner was held as usual at Mr Howe's Rooms in Uphill. Standing up at the top table are the cream of local respectability - Mr Saunders the village schoolmaster, the Rev. S.R. Hosbons, Mr B.H. Hill J.P. and Chairman, Detective Superintendent Froest who was with Scotland Yard and played a key role in capturing the murderer Dr Crippen. Standing to the left of 'Grampa' Jones (with beard) is the ubiquitous Hon. Secretary George Masters.

Uphill Castle had just been offered the new cricket ground by the Graves-Knyfton estate which was to become their permanent home. In a speech that year, honoured guest Mr G. McKenna, the Weston-super-Mare Cricket Club Chairman, pointed out that now Uphill's new ground was adjacent to the Weston pitch the rather portly players of the Uphill club would provide much needed shelter for the rather exposed Weston ground. History does not relate whether he made it home safely that night!

These dinners were always considered by the team and officials as the highlight of the club calendar. Usually held in late November or early December they feasted on boiled mutton with caper sauce and roast beef followed by Christmas pudding and mince pies and all for 5/- (25p).

Despite the usual number of distinguished guests, a few of the team always had far too much to drink because they used to meet much earlier in the Dolphin as soon as it opened (a tradition which has been handed down and is enthusiastically upheld by club members today). On one occasion a particular fellow was so inebriated that he put lashings of horseradish sauce on his Christmas pudding mistaking it for custard, much to the delight of his companions.

All the important guests and members spoke with great fervour and between each speech someone would always get to their feet and sing a solo. Renditions such as 'Pilgrim of Love' and 'Till the sands of the desert grow cold' were popular and it was quite common for these festivities to go on until three or four o'clock in the morning.

"It was quite different for men like Larwood and Voce to bowl these balls on the leg stick. They could pitch the ball within a foot of what they aimed for. It would be different when they got some village lad slinging 'em down anyhow" (hear, hear).

THE THIRTIES

Although the country was in the depths of a depression, Uphill Castle flourished modestly and because of the motor coach were able to travel in relative comfort to away matches. Indeed venues were arranged against Midsomer Norton, Chipping Sodbury and even Cardiff City Corporation.

The following report from the 11th March 1933 edition of the Weston Gazette again pays tribute to the remarkable work of the Hon. Secretary, George Masters. By his sterling efforts he had secured an incredible 84 Vice Presidents, 59 Honorary members and even 26 lady members. Not surprisingly, laughter broke out when it was announced there were only 15 playing members! There is also an intriguing commentary on how the England/Australia Body-Line controversy was being interpreted at village cricket level.

UPHILL CASTLE CRICKET CLUB
Remarkable Record on Vice-Presidents and Hon. Members
Body-Line Bowling
Happy Time Spent at The Annual Dinner

The Uphill Castle Cricket Club has built up an enviable reputation during the forty odd years of its existence, not only for the sportsmanship which always marks its games, but for the measure of practical support which it draws from the neighbourhood and from Weston. It has a list of vice-presidents and honorary members of which many a far more pretentious club would be proud, and it has a generous and enthusiastic president in Miss Graves-Knyfton, who assists the organisation in many ways. The annual dinner is an epitome of the spirit of the Club, and that which was held on Friday evening was among the most successful in its history. It was held at the School, and a company numbering about 75 gathered. Much of the continued success of the Club is due to the genial personality of Mr. George Masters, who has been honorary secretary ever since its foundation, and, like Father O'Flynn, has a "wonderful way wid him" in enrolling vice-presidents and honorary members.

The Rector of Uphill the Rev. S. R. Hosbons, made and ideal Chairman and he was supported by well-known residents of Uphill and Weston, including Messrs. R. Hosken, A.E. Lock, R.A. Riddell, F.W. Shearmur, Commander O.G. Smale, R.N., etc. Numerous letters of apology for absence were also received. Mr. George

Parker, of Waterloo street, Weston-super-Mare, undertook the catering in first-class style, and a capital musical programme interspersed the brief toast list. Those contributing were Messrs., H.J. Cottell, F. Stuckey, H.J. Blackmore, R. Hosken, C.G. Rothery, L. G. Tanner, G. Poole and Scott McAulay, together with the Uphill Glen Singers consisting of Messrs. E. Williams, H. Cottell, F. Stuckey and L. Tanner.

When Uphill Absorbs Weston!

The loyal toast having been honoured, The Chairman proposed the health of the President, Miss Graves-Knyfton, and prefaced his remarks by observing that the Weston papers had been poking fun at their church clock. One obvious advantage of the clock, however, was that although it was stopped it was right twice a day, whereas there were lots of people who were not that!. Miss Graves-Knyfton, he continued, occupied a rather unique position in as much as she was president of a men's club, and much as she would like to be present her feminine reticence kept her away. For many years, since her father's death, she had been president of Uphill Castle C.C. and an extraordinarily good club it must be to retain her as president, and so many vice-presidents. He was told by Mr. Masters, who was a sort of everlasting secretary in the same way that he was an everlasting church-warden, that Miss Knyfton spend a great deal of time and thought upon the club. Some time ago it was in a difficult position in regard to a playing field, but Miss Knyfton saw to it that they got a field, and it was still a continuous club. "We are ceasing to be a village, as we understand that Weston-super-Mare will soon belong to us", observed the Chairman amid laughter. "That is one way of putting it, but I hope that whatever happens the Uphill Castle Cricket Club will never lose its individuality. In any case I am voicing everybody's opinions when I say that Miss Knyfton is a jolly good fellow'" (applause).

Should Retain Individuality.

The toast was accorded musical honours, and Mr. R.A. Riddell replied on behalf of the president. They had in Miss Graves-Knyfton, he said, a thorough and true sportsman, one who had the village and the Cricket Club at heart. She wanted the old traditions to continue and the Uphill Castle Cricket Club to go on in a prosperous manner as it had been conducted in the past. Cricket was a game which brought young fellows together and made men and sportsmen of them; it taught them in fact, how to play the game. He supposed under the new conditions Uphill would no longer be a parish (The Chairman: "Yes, we shall be a parish"). Well, Uphill will come under the same rates and taxes as Weston-super-Mare (laughter). He hoped that Uphill would never lose its individuality, and as far as the Cricket club was concerned they could rely upon Miss Graves-Knyfton to help them in every way that was humanly possible (applause). In conclusion, Mr Riddell announced that he had been entrusted by Mrs. Graves-Knyfton with a donation towards the Club funds.

Mr. F.W. Shearmur gave "The Vice-Presidents" and extended to them grateful thanks for the very loyal support they had given the Club for so many years. Any club could be proud of such a list (hear, hear). Chief credit, he thought, was due to a certain gentleman who was getting about on three wheels. The vice-presidents and Mr. George Masters were bound up together and they would have a devil of a job to find which was which (laughter). He showed wonderful energy in persuading them to "cough up the necessary dough" on which the Club flourished. As one speaker had put it, Uphill was taking over Weston-super-Mare on the day when as boys they used to play practical jokes. On April 1 Weston would be merged with Uphill, and he asked members of the Club not to lose their identity: they would certainly not lose that comradeship which had gone on for so many years - long before he came to reside in the parish.

Mr. H.S. Blick, replying, said he found from their membership book that there were 81 vice-presidents, 59 honorary members and 28 lady members, while the actual playing members numbered fifteen (laughter). He thought that in itself testified strongly to the popularity of the playing members, and also to the activity of the honorary secretary and the successful manner in which he "drew in the dabs" (laughter).

Body-Line Bowling.

Mr. H. W. Saunders proposed the toast of "The Uphill Castle Cricket Club" and remarked that it was very nice and very refreshing in more ways than one to be present at that annual function. In the Uphill Castle Club a feeling of peace and harmony and good fellowship always existed. Particularly was this so at present, because of late they had been living in very hectic times as regarded cricket. They were delighted to know that the M.C.C. side had done so well in Australia and succeeded in winning back the ashes (hear, hear). At the same time he was quite sure all true sportsmen deplored that constant wrangling and ugly spirit which seemed to have crept into Test cricket (hear, hear). They were delighted to read the dignified reply which the M.C.C. sent to their friends in Australia and apparently for the time being that had closed the incident. He as not going to attempt to enter into the rights and wrongs of body-line bowling, but he thought it a thousand pities that so much had been said and written about it by people who had not seen or played cricket, people who had never seen an 'in swinger' or played the leg theory. One thing gave him a good deal of concern, and that was whether this was going to be the start of an epidemic among clubs and schools. If so, he thought the old game of cricket would be absolutely spoilt. It was quite different for men like Larwood and Voce to bowl these balls on the leg stick. They could pitch the ball within a foot of what they aimed for. It would be different when they got some village lad slinging 'em down anyhow (hear, hear). If that crept into local cricket the youths would not get that love of the game which they wanted to see, and therefore he hoped that schools would not foster that type of bowling (hear, hear). They had always been proud of the way in which they played cricket in this part of the country, and he hoped they would strive to keep that bowling out of club cricket. As soon as it ceased to be a game it was not worth playing . With such men at the helm as Mr. George Masters and Mr. Ernest Williams the traditions of the game would be up-held in that Club. He wished the Club every success in the future and knew that they would always play the game (applause).

George Masters

On January 16th 1934, following his customary immaculate presentation of the annual accounts George Masters announced that he wished to be relieved of the office of Hon. Secretary and treasurer. Forty years was a good run and he was beginning to feel the strain of it. He was speaking quite seriously when he said that he felt he could carry on no longer. He wished to thank the honorary members of the club for the generous support they had given to the club during those forty years. He was afraid that without that help there would have been no Uphill Castle Cricket Club.

Despite pleas by Dick Amesbury, and Arthur Hobbs as well as the Chairman, Rev. Hosbons, he had made up his mind and would not reconsider. He even proposed that Harry Minifie should take over the post.

A few weeks later, at the annual dinner held at the schoolroom in Uphill, many people paid tribute to the work George Masters had done for the club. Although he was unwell and could not attend the dinner, Miss Graves-Knyfton made a rare appearance and presented a wireless set for Mr Masters which was received on his behalf by Mr Stanley Luff.

She told the gathering that members past and present plus friends from the village has subscribed towards the presentation and, out of the large amount donated, they were going to have Mr Master's house electrically wired and the balance remaining would be handed to him in the form of a cheque. Despite his great age and the fact that he had an artificial leg made of cork, he still travelled around the village on his sturdy tricycle. He continued to take a keen interest in the clubs activities and even attended the opening of the new pavilion in 1938. He would have no doubt have been infuriated to learn a season later that someone had lost all the club's scorebooks!

He outlived his wife by 3 years and died in 1942. Outside his Uphill home, Redcliffe house, he would regularly pin up the team sheets on a Thursday evening and there would always be great interest in the names selected. This notice board is still there today and stands as a silent tribute to probably the greatest servant of Uphill Castle Cricket Club.

Redcliffe House Uphill - the home of George Masters showing the Notice Board where he used to pin up the team sheets on a Thursday evening.

The New Pavilion

In March 1938 the committee announced that they had ordered a new pavilion from Messrs Prattens of Midsomer Norton at a cost of £117. It appeared that in order to meet the clubs full specification, some minor alterations would be needed which would involve even more expense.

The pavilion duly arrived in sections and was erected in time for the first match of the season - against Congresbury.

On Saturday May 7th 1938 the new club house was officially opened by the President Miss Graves-Knyfton in front of a sizeable gathering of players and supporters. She was presented with a bouquet by Miss Audrey Cossens, daughter of the then Vice Chairman and mentioned in her speech that she had heard recently that the popularity of cricket was due to it's uncertainty of the weather, the pitch and the players, an astute observation and still very true today.

The ebullient Chairman, the Rev. S. Rowland Hobsons, responded by saying that whilst the pavilion was "a very nice bit of work" there was a "snag" and he looked to everyone present to help remove the problem. The fact that the club didn't have quite enough funds to pay for it!

The photograph shows Miss Graves-Knyfton with Rev. Hobsons behind and to her left George Masters, Joe Cossens and in the stripped blazer Cyril Savill the club hon. treasurer who had spearheaded the drive for club funds to acquire the building.

Just over a year later on July 2nd 1939 the club was burgled and the miscreants stole the gas meter which had only been installed two months earlier and contained just a few shillings. Six packets of cigarettes also went missing.

A press report at the time suggested that as the point of entry was through a small window which had been forced open it was likely that the intruder was of a 'slight stature' and the manner in which the gas pipes had been cut described as 'amateurish'!

Opening the Pavilion - 1938

".....over a couple of bottles of George's ales we not only agreed to amalgamate but also to head the fixture card Weston-super-Mare and Uphill Castle Cricket Club".

THE FORTIES

Under threatening skys from Germany, the 1940 season got underway with a reduced number of hastily arranged fixtures for just one team (a second XI having been formed a couple of years earlier). It was unanimously agreed that in order to save raw materials, as well as much needed cash, no fixture cards would be printed during the war. The committee had also recently decided to purchase a quantity of new caps in the club colours - green with a red stripe and with a white castle over the peak - so the team must have looked good even though they were only to play in a limited number of games.

One such match was against the ladies, the men having to bowl under-arm, catch with one hand and bat opposite their usual stance - a procedure that would infuriate Womens Lib activists today. Due to some quite appalling umpiring decisions the game ended in a tie!

Club matters in 1940 were still dominated by lack of funds with the treasurer, Mr Savill, working miracles trying to balance the books.

Before the war regular whist drives in the village provided a valuable source of income but these had had to be suspended because of the very strict blackout laws. Loyalties were divided as to whether any new funds from Vice Presidents should be used to pay off the debt still owing on the pavilion or go towards an even more urgent need - that of collecting for the Weston Spitfire fund (which did eventually reach it's target of £5000 in 1942).

In 1940 farmer George Edwards from Wick St.Lawrence took over the lease on Manor Farm and leased a parcel of land in the village which included the Uphill Cricket ground. Rent was fixed at a peppercorn rate and in return Mr. Edwards (who was no mean cricketer himself) was allowed to graze his sheep over the winter months. An amicable arrangement which lasted into the early fifties when the lease reverted back to an agreement direct with Miss Graves-Knyfton.

During the war years the cricket pavilion was used as unofficial base for the local home guard and there was always keen attendance particularly when special manoeuvres were arranged. On one such occasion the home guard battalion was split into two teams and a serious war 'game' planned. It was scheduled to start at 6.00 pm and George Edwards who was in one of the teams was busily milking his cows so that he could be ready on time.

Suddenly the cow shed door burst open and in walked the enemy with their rifles levelled at the luckless farmer. Protesting unsuccessfully that they had cheated by starting early he was marched off to the Uphill cricket pavilion and incarcerated there with the rest of his side who had also been rounded up in the "pre-match swoop".

By some strange coincidence there was a considerable quantity of alcohol stored in the club house and when 'the prisoners' were eventually released late in the afternoon on the following day all the stock had been consumed - no doubt considered as essential rations!

The cricket field provided a good source of hay in the summer months as no games were played on the home ground after 1940. Unfortunately, the fornicating activities of American servicemen infuriated the farm workers, not so much because they were jealous of our American cousins, but their discarded condoms would jam up the cutters of the mowers. As if to serve as a warning to would be trespassers, the farm hands used to hang the spent condoms in rows on the barbed wire fence at the entrance to the ground!

The indomitable F.J. Cossens who was Chairman of Uphill Castle Cricket Club from 1939 to 1963.

Memories of Weston and Uphill Cricket Club

- by Syd Hayward
President Weston-super-Mare Cricket Club

Old age memory like an out of form batsman often fails to register but just as the batsman eventually returns to form, so does the memory.

It is then with very great pleasure that I stretch my memory back well over fifty years to the happy and successful amalgamation of the Weston-super-Mare and Uphill Cricket Clubs. Unfortunately this entails reminiscing, writing of characters that players of today never knew or even heard of. But it was those worthy characters of yesteryear who built the Uphill Club into a fine village side and kept the flag flying in the war time 'forties', Fred Taylor, Harry Taylor, Joe Cossens, Charlie Peverelle, Dick Amesbury, Cyril Savill, R.T. Wilding and Chris Smith and may I be forgiven if my memory has failed even one other stalwart.

In the early forties so many players of both clubs were being 'called up' into the Forces that it was about as difficult week by week to pick a settled side as it was then to buy a bottle of Scotch.

So a meeting was arranged with the Uphill skipper Dick Amesbury in the old wooden pavilion on the Weston ground where over a couple of bottles of George's ales we not only agreed to amalgamate but also to head the fixture card Weston-super-Mare and Uphill Castle Cricket Club.

Thus began a very happy and successful association with so many Uphill players giving unstinted service.

Of them all I am bound to mention Chris Smith. What a bowler! While his grip on the ball could best be described as 'crablike', he began his 'run up' like an out of step guardsman. Stuttering to the wicket as though trying to regain some sort of rhythm he ended up by bowling off the wrong foot!

But there the comedy finished and the drama began, for when the ball pitched it did not just deviate as most off spinners hope to achieve, it turned sharply. There was no such finesse as change of pace or flight but simply unremitting line, length and spin. In normal times Chris could have graced top grade cricket and if the reader senses exaggeration let him digest the performance of Chris in the Jubilee game between the two clubs in 1943 which he will read at the end of this short tale of war time cricket.

Now the local Mercury of August 1943 takes on the story:-

A match was arranged with Weston to commemorate the Jubilee, and as most of the present members were in the Forces, we sent out an SOS to various members within travelling distance, calling on them to don their flannels again. The call was answered right manfully and eight of the old members came along, one, Mr. Harry Taylor, not having played for 29 years.

GREAT TRADITION

Included in the team was Mr. Colin Frith, grandson of Mrs. Graves-Knyfton, and it was appropriate that a member of the Graves-Knyfton family should be in the team for the occasion.

Had it not been for the war, it had been hoped to make great plans for the Club for much of its later success had been due to the immense amount of work put in by the treasurer Mr. C.H. Savill, now in the R.A.F.

"I expect you saw Charles Peverelle at the match on Saturday", said Mr. Wilding. "He lost his sight through enemy action in 1941, but he is still able to follow cricket with the aid of a running commentary, and with his own expert knowledge he can complete the mental picture with amazing accuracy".

"During his playing membership up to 1939, we always selected 'Pev' for his sure hands saved many runs and dismissed many a batsman who sent a skier in his direction. We shall miss Pev".

So there it is, fifty years of England's favourite sport (may football fans forgive me!) as portrayed by a local club, whose courage and sporting instinct has built up an unbreakable tradition, with a village and an old manor for its setting.

UPHILL CASTLE'S JUBILEE

Uphill Castle CC celebrate their Jubilee this summer and to help in the commemoration, the Weston Club are going to play a special match against them on Saturday, Sept 3rd. When war broke out, the Weston Club agreed to co-opt with the Uphill Club for the duration, so that there should be no lapse in the continuity.

Followers of both teams are cordially invited to the Devonshire Road ground on the occasion of this game. Several Uphill Castle players have assisted Weston in the past and rendered valuable service. It is in appreciation of this, coupled with the fact of the longstanding foundation of Uphill Club, that we hope for a good crowd.

OLD TIMERS

Many spectators and followers of both teams met at the Devonshire Road ground to see battle done. Both sides had available crowds of players - old and young - and in the end it was decided to put 13 men on each side. 'Pon my word! it was a sight to see'em".

It was a real delight too to see so many old time Weston players present, Ned Sainsbury (his son played for Uphill), Charlie Pinton and many old village war horses. The yarns they swopped was music to the ears of cricket lovers. One really lived in the past for a while. What days those were to be sure! but that's not the record of the match.

Weston won the toss and batted. Somehow, Chris Smith, the Uphill Castle bowler, who has played and bowled so well for Weston this season, had the time of his life and bowled so well that in the end he had taken 10 wickets for 10 runs! Twice he missed the hat-trick and, until the last pair of Weston batsmen got together, he had the remarkable figures of 8 for 5!

Weston had 10 wickets down for 36, and this was when Pickering was out for 24 of them. Young Sainsbury had taken over the attack from the opening bowler Wilding, when Pickering was 2, and the batsman took a fancy to the attack at once and promptly collected 13 off his first over. Pinnock and Syd Hayward were the last two in and they carried the score to 52 before Smith bowled Hayward for 9. It was an exciting last wicket stand. Pinnock was not out 7.

Tea was taken and during this interval various guesses were made as to the result.

REMARKABLE COLLAPSE

Once again, cricket proved its uncertainty. No good trying to forecast decisions. No game of cricket is won till it is lost. Uphill's reply was remarkable for its collapse. They were put out for 19! 13 out for 19, and all this owing to the remarkable bowling of Noake and Collett.

Both were in excellent form, and the latter, who played his last game before going into the services, never bowled better. Noake took 7 for a dozen runs and in his second over, did the hat-trick when he got the wickets of Frith, C.W. Wood and Miles. Only 5 runs had been scored. Collett finished up with 5 for 5.

The home sides fielding was good throughout. It was a great finish to a good season, for out of 17 matches played, 8 were won, 7 lost, 1 drawn, and 2 abandoned. The young players available and their enthusiasm are most encouraging, and justifies to the full any efforts put forward by the club officials to keep the game going.

Saturday's full scores were as follows:-

Weston-super-Mare

I.J. Fraser b. Smith	1
W.D. Hayward lbw. B. Smith	4
P. Baldwin c. Young b. Smith	0
J. Pickering b. Smith	24
E.H. Statham lbw. b. Smith	0
L.V. Noakes b. Sainsbury	0
R. Searle c. Sainsbury b. Smith	0
A. Hughes b. Smith	0
N. Board b. Smith	0
T. Howell c. C. Wood b. Smith	1
N. Pinnock not out	7
D. Collett c. Young b. Sainsbury	0
S. Hayward b. Smith	9
extras	6
Total	**52**

Uphill

C.D. Frith lbw. Noakes	2
T.G. Young c. Statham b. Collett	9
C.W. Wood b. Noakes	0
G. Miles b. Noakes	0
R.T.R. Lewis b. Noakes	0
C. Smith b. Collett	2
J.P. Sainsbury b. Noakes	1
H. Hart c. Searle b. Noakes	3
E. Porter b. Noakes	0
H. Taylor c. W.D. Hayward b. Collett	0
R. Amesbury b. Collett	0
W.G. Wood b. Collett	0
R.T. Wilding not out	0
extras	2
Total	**19**

May I, on behalf of the Weston-super-Mare Cricket Club wish Uphill Castle Cricket Club a very happy, prosperous and successful centenary year in 1993.

FLOREAT UPHILL CASTLE C.C.

The late forties saw the club getting back to full strength, running two regular senior sides and the emergence of a highly successful youth side.

Uphill Castle Junior XI - Winners of League Championship Season 1950
B.J. Bush J. Wormleighton M.R. Bees B. Lewis B. Browning J. R. Atkin D. Prosser P. Taylor
G. Stocker R.V. Berkeley D.W. Price A.J. Trott B.J. Scott B.E. Fry M.J. Farr

Uphill Castle C.C. 1949.

F.W. Parker (Hon.Sec.) - A. Berkeley - F.E. Brown - M.J. Ree - R. Evans (Scorer 1st XI) B.E. Fry E. Bateman O. Smith M.J. Farr
R.V. Berkeley F. Cresswell T. Whittington
D.Evans N.Tench J. Slocombe C. Bagg E.V. Fry C. Thomas C. Savill (hon Treasurer)
E. Philputt (match sec) R.L. Bucknell (capt) Mr E. Llewelyn (vice chairman) H. Greenwood (capt 2XI) R. Amesbury
W. Popham (vice capt 1st XI) Mr F.J. Cossens (chairman) E. Salvage (vice capt 2XI) M.P. Watts

"Lolloping in, delivery arm high, left leg extended he propelled the ball at a speed envied by us youngsters, only to be straight driven back over his head and out of the ground"

THE FIFTIES
- by Gordon Porter

It was certainly a different club in the 50's compared to today. At the ground, the existing pavilion was there, but no tea hut, shower, garage, or flush toilets and no mechanical roller. The small dressing rooms in the rear of the pavilion allowed changing in shifts, it being reminiscent of a Charlie Chaplin film. When you found your trousers, odds on someone else was wearing them. Meals were provided in the front of the pavilion with the ladies working wonders in cramped conditions.

At the start of the decade Uphill were already running a successful youth side winning the Junior League Championship in 1949 and 1950 and which provided the senior sides with a host of talent. Most of the youngsters soon left the district, the youth team eventually folded and hasn't been revised to date. Nevertheless, Uphill ran two sides with many outstanding players, capable of challenging most local clubs.

Throughout the fifties Uphill's fortunes seemed to mirror that of Somerset's - a great team to watch, full of characters but with seemingly terminal financial problems. Indeed at the annual general meeting in 1954 it was stated that the measure of financial support would determine "the life or death of the club" - depressing stuff!

Although it's well over forty years since my first game for Uphill I can still vividly recall my first match. After losing the toss we took the field and ten minutes later after our opening attack had failed to make any impact on the opposition, our skipper pointed to me and said "next over please George" luckily Ernie Bateman explained that my name was Gordon Porter and I was supposed to be an opening batsman/wicket-keeper!! Goodness knows who he thought I was. Perhaps Ernie ought to have said nothing and maybe I could have been Uphill's Alec Bedser!

Travelling to away matches was always by coach, except my first captain who went by car - shades of Gentlemen and Players, as far as I recall he was probably the only player with his own vehicle. However, as the affluent society came along cars became the general mode of transport.

Fixtures started and ended with Burnham, and on Bank Holiday Mondays we played all day matches against Wiveliscombe. One Sunday match on the fixture list was the away game against Weston - always hard fought. Kit was still being provided by the Club, and was available even as players were able to produce their own.

As now 'The Castle' were indebted in the 50's to a few members who worked hard on and off the field.

The 60's approached with a more relaxed attitude in running the club, improvements to the facilities in the offing, and some exciting moments to come in Uphill's history.

Old Faithful

The faithful clubhouse as most people would like to remember it - without the hideous backdrop of the current edifice. This picture was taken in the tea interval during a match in 1950.

Although vastly over-shadowed in size by the new Weston Cricket pavilion which was to open four years later, this delightful little building has now served the club admirably for well over 50 years.

Bill Andrews and Uphill Castle
- *by Mike Farr*

Bill Andrews played for Uphill Castle in the late forties and early fifties after one of the numerous times he had been discarded by Somerset.

Mike Farr who was then a young and impressionable fast bowler from Weston Grammar School reminisces about his experience with the legendary local hero.

"Bill Andrews was the guru of us youngsters, and when coaching, to encourage our bowling he would put a half-crown on the off stump, take guard and 'arrange' to miss a straight one. I'm fairly sure it was claimed on a rota!

When doing groundsman duties one year, he got us collecting the droppings from the sheep which had been grazing on the ground in winter and we put the whole mess in a large metal drum. Bill then prepared a slurry which was spread over the square and rolled level. For some time the square was brownish, shone in the sun and no ball ever turned or bounced.... until it got wet! then it was devastating. I have never come across this practice since, probably for a very good reason!"

The following headline and story from the Bristol Evening World sounded full of promise and optimism for Uphill Castle.

Bill Andrews To Take a Special Team to Bath

"Bill" Andrews, Somerset cricketer, is to take a Special XI of the Uphill Castle C.C., Weston-super-Mare, to Hampsett, Bath, on Saturday to celebrate the opening of a new ground there.

The Uphill Castle team will include, in addition to W.H.R. Andrews (capt), L. Angell also of the Somerset County Club.

Team will be: Andrews, C. Thomas, Angell, Dr. R. Alford, E. Bateman, R.V. Berkeley, R. Bucknell, F.E. Brown, M.J. Farr, B. Pike, C. Savill, Reserve R. Whittington.

Coach leaves Uphill Castle ground at 12.30 p.m.

In reality, however things turned out rather different.

"The Hampsett openers were untroubled by us youngsters who opened the bowling. Bill then decided enough was enough and took off a short run. Runs came faster. He then announced rather loudly that he was going to redirect the course of events by bowling off his long run (but not exactly in those words!).

Lolloping in, delivery arm high, left leg extended he propelled the ball at a speed envied by us youngsters, only to be straight driven back over his head and out of the ground - it was some time before the ball was recovered, the ground being at the top of the hill.

What happened was, I believe, our first experience that cricket can be a very serious business!

Bill Andrews ran a successful sports shop business in Uphill village for some time and one day I remember sitting in my bedroom window watching Bill with Johnny Lawrence trying out the then new plastic ball in the middle of Old Church road. Such traffic, as there was, obligingly stopped if it's arrival was inconvenient.

Speaking of traffic, Bill's car driving was legendary. He reckoned it was safest to drive with the car bonnet mascot directly in line with the cats eyes in the middle of the road and he could then navigate country lanes at speed with the door open, one hand on the steering wheel while the other ensured the lads in the back did not get sprayed!! (If you get my drift).

His advice to his young admirers (and we owed much of our love of cricket to him) was to have two pints before a game, because one slops around.

Us youngsters literally lived at the ground in the summer, practising, helping to prepare wickets, catching eels in the river, even watching courting couples in the adjacent field. I have many happy memories of those days as an Uphill junior - not least being introduced to responsible drinking".

Reprinted from the Bill Andrew's Column,
Bristol Evening World,
Saturday August 22nd 1959.

On Sunday I played against Uphill Castle. One of the oldest clubs in the district, and they have had a really good season - losing only two matches. Their strength seems to lie in their batting and Gordon Porter has been very consistent at No.1 and has scored over 500 runs.

Jack Bickell, although getting near the veteran stage hits the ball hard through the covers. Trevor Osbourne, a left-hand batsman, looked in form and he is a competent wicket-keeper. John Sperring is the skipper of the Castle side, and in addition to making runs has been taking wickets with his off "tweakers".

Roy Meade another ex-pace bowler is still hitting the ball hard and so is Brian Parker. I like the left-hand batting of 16 year old Geoff Hazzard, who is one of Syd Hayward's boys.

Ernie Bateman has again been making a lot of runs and his 91 against Bridgwater Cellophane was chanceless.

A match in progress in the early fifties

Uphill Castle 1st XI - 1958

J. Bickell R. Bucknell R. Shaw R. Meade G. Porter B. Parker
B. Stoneham C. Thomas J. Sperring J. Partridge C. Smith

"The best wickets are on the pavilion side of the square"

THE SIXTIES

In the late 50's and early 60's many of the immediate post war team such as Chris Smith, Ernie Bateman, Cyril Thomas and Dick Bucknell were coming to the end of their long playing days. Later in the decade new cricketers arrived such as Mike Hughes, Tony Slocombe, Mike Turnbull and Derek Brown and all were to play a significant part in successfully leading the club through the difficult transition from playing all friendly matches to a regular league programme.

To an outsider, the early 60's at Uphill Castle must have portrayed the image of a rather select and austere association, reminiscent of a rather élite gentleman's society. Anyone wishing to join the club really had to make themselves known to an official and then had to complete a written application form with probing questions, such as details of career structure, as well as cricketing experience and ability. This document was submitted to the executive committee headed by Joe Cossens for scrutiny who then decided if the applicant had suitable credentials!

Prospective candidates who passed this first test were then invited by letter to a players meeting where they could be formally introduced to the club officials and captains. Having got over this hurdle successfully a further letter was sent "granting" membership. This particular communication was known officially as a "Notice of acceptance of membership". Rules of engagement were relaxed a little from 1964 when Bill Popham took up the Chairmanship and Joe was offered the honorary post of Deputy President - a unique position within Uphill Castle that had never before or since been assigned. Joe Cossens remained deputy President until his sad and untimely death in a car accident at Bleadon some years later.

In 1968 the club celebrated it's 75th anniversary, and to mark the occasion a special match was arranged against an invitation XI, drawing players from all the local clubs in the district. It turned out to be an excellent afternoon's cricket with many former players and club officials amongst the spectators.

Uphill Castle in the Sixties

- by Chris Twort
(Uphill Castle, 1964 - 1967)

Now in charge of cricket at Millfield Junior School

My first years playing for the Castle were in 1964/1965 when I was captain of the local Grammar School side and in those seasons there was a strong link between the Club and the school staff, several of whom were playing members. Indeed, the Midweek XI often contained as many as seven or eight school teachers, especially when Doug Marshall was skipper. Doug was a fanatical Welshman who taught Biology at the school and who looked after their Under-12 cricket team. On a famous day in 1965, Uphill Primary School (whose side included one Nick Evans) bowled Doug's team out for TWO. Doug refused to enter the staff room the following day, fearful of the jibes and feeling safer in his lab.

I well remember playing in a midweek game for the Castle when the Town Hall were the the opposition in a friendly fixture. They were captained by Gordon Porter, one of Uphill's most distinguished former players and a great worker for the Club. Keeping wicket, I caught Gordon down the leg-side and, without waiting for a possible appeal, he set off for the pavilion. I'm sure that Gordon always walked if he knew he was out.

What other memories of a quarter of a century ago? Jack Bickell, another stalwart member and no mean player, cutting the outfield, driving a contraption which I never knew how he got started; John Sperring, a fine off-spinner and batsman, opening the innings one day so he could then go off and visit his wife in hospital where she was about to give birth; those memorable teas of Joy Porter and Babs Bickell.

League cricket hadn't arrived in the sixties, but I'm sure that didn't stop us pulling out all the stops when trying to win. One of the best - and unluckiest - bowlers I kept to was Brian Parker, who had the ability to move the ball late and so often beat the outside edge. It was the same with John Scott when I moved across the road to play for Weston.

I enjoyed playing at Uphill Castle's picturesque ground where Gordon Robert once hit the ball over the tallest tree. It seems incredible but I was there! "The best wickets are on the pavilion side of the square", Gordon Porter once confided to me. I don't know if this is still the case, but I do know that the Club appears to be thriving and in good shape. Long may this continue.

The Great Match

by Jack Bickell

WESTON SUNDAY XI v
UPHILL CASTLE SUNDAY XI
at DEVONSHIRE ROAD - 19.8.62

In their annual Sunday fixture against Weston, Uphill Castle produced a shock and freak result that can only be described as "That's Cricket". It must not only rank as the most convincing win of the season for Uphill Castle, but probably also in the history of the club.

Weston fielded an almost full strength side, (indeed at least three of whom had had Somerset County experience), and were dismissed for a mere 15 runs against an Uphill Castle side that were normally considered to be of Weston's 2nd XI standard.

Uphill Castle were put into bat and managed to reach 122 for 9 before declaring, Gordon Porter (33) and Dick Shaw (28) putting on a respectable 51 for the first wicket. The middle order struggled but thanks to John Sperring (23 not out) and Brian Parker (11 not out) took the total to 122 for 9 declared.

Then came the rout. The Uphill Castle opening attach of Colin Hawkins 4 for 4 and Brian Parker 5 for 8 whipped through the Weston Batting in 14 overs. At 15 for 9 the Uphill Castle Skipper Trevor Osborne made a "tactical" change bringing on Dick Shaw who with his second ball dismissed the last man and Weston were all out for 15.

Scorecard

Uphill Castle

G. Porter c. Allison, b. Sparkes	33
R. Shaw lbw. b. Bryant	28
B. Stoneham b. Skate	3
J. Partridge b. Pitman	6
J. Bickell c. Skate b. Sparkes	0
J. Sperring n.o.	23
T. Osborne b. Webb	8
R. Meade b. Webb	0
R. Valentine b. Skate	3
C. Hawkins b. Bryant	1
B. Parker n.o.	11
extras	6
Total *(for 9 wkts. dec.)*	**122**

Weston-Super-Mare

W. Allison b. Hawkins	1
T. Willetts b. Parker	1
J. Ricketts b. Hawkins	0
D. Norton b. Hawkins	0
D. Evans c. Osborne b. Parker	5
J. Pitman b. Parker	0
C. Rose b. Parker	0
E. Bryant c&b. Parker	2
A. Webb b. Hawkins	0
T. Sparkes n.o.	0
A. Skate c. Parker b. Shaw	3
extras	3
Total	**15**

Robert Hicks M.P.

I had five very enjoyable seasons at Uphill in the late 1960's. The cricket was of good club standard and the companionship excellent. Naturally it was always better if the side had won - for a start the older players were often less inclined to bore their colleagues with exaggerated claims of past heroics - but the beer and conversation flowed freely even if we had lost.

In my day Gordon Porter certainly led from the front - a devoted servant of the club as was his brother Roy, our umpire. Jack Bickell's contributions on and off the field were legendary, Frank O'Brien's thick edge masterly - he undoubtedly saved more runs with his excellent fielding than ever came from the middle of the bat, in Mike Hughes and Brian Parker the club possessed a pair of opening bowlers of genuine quality (in 5 years I never actually discovered what Mike actually did at Westlands although I was soon told the secret of Brian's success!).

It is now over 20 years ago that I last played for Uphill. The fact that I can still recall vividly the personalities and incidents bear testimony to the happy years spent "dropping catches in the slips" or "yawning in the midfield" in that beautiful setting with the knowledge that the ladies would provide the best cricket teas I have known, and afterwards there would be the bonus of a few pints of Badgers.

Congratulations to Uphill Castle on achieving your centenary - may you continue you innings for many years to come.

Thank you for the pleasure you have given to so many over the years.

UPHILL CASTLE CC 75th ANNIVERSARY MATCH AUGUST 3 1968

J. Bickell, R. Hicks, G. Wagner, R. Davidson, J. Hooper, J. Sperring, T. Maher, F. O'Brien, M. Hughes, W. Popham (Chairman), G. Porter(Captain), D. Bryant

"The odd leg spinner mixed with the gently-rolled off spinners, caused havoc..."

THE SEVENTIES

The 1970's marked the introduction of a major change in cricket at Uphill. The Somerset cricket league was founded in 1973 and after a lively players meeting later that year it was agreed that Uphill Castle should apply to join.

Although there had been some earlier opposition, it was generally felt that the club would actually have difficulty in finding reasonable fixtures as most other teams in the area were also joining with the league.

It was obvious that, like it or not, competitive league cricket was here to stay and clubs not participating would eventually lose their most talented players and would therefore no longer be able to field an effective team.

So in 1974, Uphill Castle, together with approximately 25 other clubs, played in an enlarged division to determine who would form the 2nd and 3rd divisions which were to commence in 1975. Fixtures for this year were made by participating clubs and a minimum amount of matches had to be arranged between them. Final positions were based on percentage points per game and those who finished in the top twelve, which included Uphill, formed division 2.

In the long hot summer of 1976 under the expert guidance of Mike Hughes, Uphill won the division and gained deserved promotion to division 1 and this status was easily retained for many years with the club occupying a comfortable mid-table position each year.

Under the astute captaincy of Tony Slocombe the 2nd XI also developed a liking for league cricket and gained promotion for themselves within the combination league during the late 70's.

There are, of course, dozens of stories of gallantry and heroics and probably all worthy of space here, at least the participants would agree, but in a lighter vein a particularly funny moment happened during a 2nd XI game at Stothert and Pitt in Bath - one of their larger batsmen strode out to the wicket and asked for a 'one leg' guard. The Stothert umpire said 'to the off a bit - a bit more - too much - back a bit, back a bit more - that's one leg'. The hefty player looked quizzically down at this bat, then at the umpire and said in a loud voice 'That's where I had it in the first place you ——— doughnut!' The Uphill fielders collapsed in a heap of laughter.

Another year later at the same venue, (it's the one where visiting fielders count the number of idiots shouting "Howzat!" from the passing trains) a groundsman was up a ladder whitewashing a huge corrugated fence to one end of the field.

All of a sudden the tranquillity of the game was interrupted by a noise like a machine gun as the ladder slipped sideways with gathering speed against the corrugated sheeting. The poor groundsman still clinging helplessly at the top of the ladder crashed onto the grass and splattered himself in whitewash.

The game was temporarily halted while we ensured there were no broken bones and he limped off red-faced and embarrassed to the pavilion to shower and change.

Undeterred he returned to his task half an hour later only to repeat the performance but this time completely soaking himself in the whitewash!

As the 70's progressed the club committee began to realise that the general facilities for the home and visiting teams were quite poor compared to those offered by many opposing grounds.

It was the herculean efforts of Derek Patch who instigated much of the rebuilding work which the club still enjoys to this day. Derek, with his unstinting energy reorganised the pavilion, put in showers, erected the garage and provided the club's first mechanical roller.

In those days the home square was still relatively small with only six tracks side by side so most Sunday matches were played away. Even so with a full season of Saturday fixtures it needed Gordon Porter's careful husbandry and manipulation to produce a good wicket every week.

Uphill Castle's match reports reached new dizzy heights on 22nd June 1975. The ultimate accolade was this short feature written by Eric Hill which appeared in the Telegraph sitting proudly next to match summaries on England Vs. West Indies, Northants Vs. Notts, Leicester Vs. Hampshire and Somerset Vs. Warwickshire.

Even this short prose demonstrates pure eloquence and erudition, characteristics which don't normally trouble bleary-eyed skippers hastily penning their match reports on a Monday morning to meet local newspaper deadlines.

Uphill win spin battle

- by Eric Hill

Brian Chetwynde of Uphill Castle heavily underlined the value of a slow spinner in limited over cricket, taking six for 35 as his side won handsomely by 89 runs in the Somerset League match at Wiveliscombe.

Uphill owed their formidable 158 for seven in the statutory 45 overs to two partnerships. Turnbull hooking and square cutting eagerly and defending very straight, made an accomplished 60 as the foundation, having been dropped when 28.

Whaites, breaking out of desperate early difficulties, counter-attacked lustily in a stand of 64, then after Knight and the off-spinner Farley had caused middle order problems, Curry swung a cheerful and important 33 runs.

The baked pitch offered bounce and turn all through. Now steady bowling based on some fascinating slow spinning by Chetwynde, backed by safe catching, starting with a brilliant effort from Giles, soon caused deep inroads in Wiveliscombe's disappointing batting.

Sprague made a spirited 24 before being caught in the deep and attempts to flog Chetwynde out of sight brought regular wickets, Bickell accepting one fine boundary catch.

The odd leg spinner mixed with the gently-rolled off spinners, caused havoc, Uphill Castle ending with a richly deserved points advantage of 18 - 3.

Reproduced by kind permission of the Daily Telegraph

The First XI 1976

R. Porter (umpire), P. Maffey, R. Curry, D. Rundell, S. Darlaston, D. Bickell, D. Patch, D. Hemming, F. O'Brien, M. Hughes (Captain), M. Turnbull, D. Reardon

2nd XI team that won promotion to Division 2 of the Somerset League - August 1979

Standing: D. Brown, D. Hall, C Wallis-Newport, R. Curry, J. Nipper, J. Prosser, D. Cook

Seated: P. Whaites, D. Harding, A. Slocombe (Captain), R. Tuort (Vice), G. Porter, A Topliss, (umpire)

.....there was little doubt in the minds of those present that David saw the poor unfortunate Somertonians as substitute Argentinian invaders.

THE EIGHTIES

The 1980's were a roller coaster for the fortunes of Uphill Castle, both on and off the field and culminating at the end of the decade with the emergence of a powerful first XI which percolated success and enthusiasm right down to the newly formed 4th XI.

Emulating Somerset from a decade earlier, a tactical declaration in September 1986 incurred the wrath of the Somerset League Committee and they withheld the First's promotion to division one in favour of Winscombe. An artificial situation that righted itself on merit a mere twelve months later.

In a way this misdemeanour seemed to encapsulate the spirit of the eighties. It was as if the club was going through a kind of wayward adolescence. Block memberships for dubious night clubs were viewed almost as valuable as club kit and extraordinary wild parties after (and sometimes before, and even occasionally during) matches were considered de rigueur.

Everyone was terrified and highly respectful of BORIS the club pig whose huge empty carcass was filled to the brim every weekend with money 'donated' by players committing the most trivial offences on or off the field.

These 'kangaroo' courts raised many hundreds of pounds every year and culminated in a massive end of season 'gentleman's 'evening' when on more than one occasion the restaurant resembled the aftermath of explosion in a fruit and vegetable market in Beirut.

Failure to score was even worse. Everyone, yes everyone in the club wore the dreaded girdle at least once, no one escaped. The offending article was discovered, strangely, in one of the changing rooms at an away game and was adopted by the club and used as punishment for anyone failing to trouble the scorers.

The miscreant had to wear the garment together with some pretty disgusting accessories and was then photographed for posterity as permanent evidence of the players' incompetence. As time went by further penalties were added and the ritual was finally abandoned only when certain forfeits became questionable in law!

On the 29th June 1985 the moon appeared for the first time and at midnight a cricket match began against the Druids (who else!) Not surprisingly, our main sponsors for the evening, Holsten Pils, saw the event develop into a huge success as large quantities of their product were dispensed amongst the two teams as well as a sizable crowd, some even watching in nearby bushes. The moon is still there today, smiling down like a wise old sage as if to mimic Father Thyme at a much grander venue. There was however a serious side to the midnight game as enough money was raised by marketing a sort of match brochure to cover the event which enabled the club to make a donation of several hundred pounds to Bristol Children's Hospital.

Amid all this social mayhem, it was left to Gareth Williams to grasp the club captaincy in 1987 and lead by clear example to bring the side up from division 2 to division 1 in 1988 and then deservedly into the Premier Division in 1990.

A thoroughly aggressive batsman who can inflict wanton destruction on an opposing bowling attack but still know precisely when to play straight and defensive. Even if it were possible to disregard these brilliant qualities his sheer optimism alone would be enough to win matches. He continues to be a tremendous influence within the club.

Brian Johnston, the doyen of the BBC cricket commentators, discussed Uphill Castle Cricket Club's midnight game live on Test Match Special during a lull in the proceedings of a test match between England and Australia at Lords in June 1985.

Memories of the Eighties

- by Brian Swift

I only had the pleasure of playing for Uphill Castle over a couple of years in the late seventies and early eighties before my evacuation to Africa (even Australia would not accept me).

However, my memories of Uphill are all happy ones as there were less politics than in other clubs, although I must say a few members had forgotten to laugh!

This matter was soon addressed with the help of those well known quick single experts C. Wallis-Newport and Dick Harvey and amongst others I was privileged to play with were Derek Patch, my subtle Captain, who could eat more fish, chips and pie than anyone I have ever met.

With Newport at first slip and me behind the stumps, I think we put more batsman off their concentration than take actual wickets. I am now totally deaf in my right ear from enforced listening to many hours of highly trivial comments from Wally.

Incidentally he also taught me to plough, once missing a corner while driving across the Mendips. He had been demonstrating the intricacies of preparing a 'roll-up' at the time.

With Roy "Sorry Son" Porter and Alf Topliss we had no problem with finding umpires, although dear Mrs Topliss used to worry a lot when she would see Alf disappear with the team for the best part of a Saturday.

It is good to see the ground and club in such a good state. We never could have fielded 4 Saturday teams in those days. That in itself pays tribute to the management of the club.

It was probably for the best that I had been deported before the arrival of Roger Fry. That combination could have been too deadly a mixture.

Best wishes from darkest Africa - I'll be thinking of you.

- *and Charles Wallis-Newport*
2nd XI Skipper (Uphill Castle C.C.)
part - 1984; 1985; 1986; 1987.

At the beginning of the Eighties, the fortunes of the first and second elevens varied considerably - with the quest for permanent promotion, by both sides, proving elusive. For example, whilst early promotion to Division 1 was achieved by the first XI, under Mike Hughes, there followed four further club skippers in rapid succession, which culminated in inevitable demotion to Division 2 in 1983.

Initially, the second eleven fared little better since, although promotion was achieved on two occasions between 1979 and 1982, the team was unable to consolidate and prompt relegation to the divisions below occurred in the seasons which immediately followed.

However, in terms of Uphill's growing enthusiasm for league cricket, it must be said that there can be no better example than the second XI of the mid-to-late 1980's! At a time when the first XI had experienced numerous changes in captaincy, and struggled to find an identity, the seconds progressed in rapid succession from half-way down Division 3 to the very top of Division 1 - in just 13 months; namely from April 1985 to May 1986. Indeed of the 45 league matches played in that time only 5 were lost - those being against the second elevens of the top premier division clubs.

A number of "memorable second eleven highlights" stand out from the past decade; "celebration Pizza" in Bristol following the end of season match against Stothert & Pitt in 1985, and also the magnificent team effort at Winscombe, twelve months later, when a winning draw in the last game the 1986 season took the team into Division 1 for the very first time.

Dave Reardon's battling 65 at Somerton in 1982, as his erstwhile colleagues in the Fleet Air Arm practised hair-raising low level flying overhead. The campaign to recover the Falkland Islands was then at it's height, and there was little doubt in the minds of those present that David saw the poor unfortunate Somertonians as substitute Argentinian invaders.

In a slightly different vein, but no less important to Uphill Castle, was the legendary "Battle of Ilminster Creek", two years later, when Andre Cox destroyed the opposition with a superb 9 wickets for 27 runs in less than ten overs! Another great moment in the "History of Sport" was Gary Slocombe's league hat trick achieved at Wells, over two weekends, in June 1986. Having taken the last two Street wickets the previous Saturday, Gary immediately clean bowled the Wells opening batsman with the very first ball of the innings!

Finally, there is one particular person who above all others deserves a very special mention. I need hardly say that the person in question is the altogether splendid Roger Fry, whom the club has honoured on more than one occasion for his major contributions over the past ten years.

It is with such thoughts, therefore, that I bring my narrative to a close.

Yours in the interest of Cricket, the club and the individual player.

The 1st XI 1984

P. Loud, A. Cox, S. Tanner, M. Mansbridge, C. Nelson, P. Evans, D. Harding, G. Board, D. Bickell, D. Patch (Captain), S. Teale, P. Griffiths.

The 2nd XI 1984

Standing:
A. Topliss (Umpire), D. Harding, R. Fry, R. Curry, M. Baxter, P. Whaites, T, Moy, J. Rowley, P, Loud.

Sitting:
G. Slocombe, C. Wallis-Newport (Captain), J. Mansbridge, N. Fletcher (Scorer).

"...tell her I'm in and I'll call her back when I'm out"

THE NINETIES

Sadly, 1992 saw the end of an incredible innings. It is quite phenomenal to record that Miss Graves-Knyfton was elected President of Uphill Castle in May 1919 and remained in office until her death in September 1992. Although few people within the club today had been acquainted with Miss Graves-Knyfton one always felt a sense of security and well-being with her name as a figure-head of the club.

Unfortunately time does not permit a more thorough obituary but no doubt future club historians will make known in greater detail the influence that she bestowed upon the club, not least by ensuring it's very existence for over seventy years.

In maintaining close links with the Graves-Knyfton estate it is particularly appropriate that her nephew Lt. Col. C.D.C. Frith OBE was unanimously elected President of Uphill Castle Cricket Club on November 6th 1992 and the management committee wish him a long and happy association with the club.

Now it's time for the current players to speak for themselves, those at the helm of the firsts and fourths, the colonial, the senior citizen and even the custodian of the wicket - all happy to tell a tale or two or put their point of view.

Perhaps the very epitome of the clubs character is summed up by the camaraderie patently evident on the nervous nineties tours. It's a happy accident that these tours are equally represented by members of each of the four league sides. One of the tour matches has been singled out and is summarised later by the 1992 master of ceremonies.

A view from the top...

- by Gareth Williams
Captain 1st XI Uphill Castle

As Uphill Castle Cricket Club enters its centenary, I am about to start my 9th year with the club, and my 7th as Captain.

I have thoroughly enjoyed my time as club captain, and it will be a privilege to hold the office during the centenary season.

During the relatively short period that I have been with Uphill, I have seen many changes occur both on and off the pitch. On Saturdays we now run 4 sides as opposed to two when I started and the club's playing strength has improved immensely. The first XI have gone from division 2 to the premier league, and our 2nd XI have made promotion from Division 3 to 1 of the 2nd XI competition. The thirds were formed in 1986 and joined the Somerset league in division 5 two years ago and have since been promoted in successive seasons, next season they will be in the same division as our 2nd XI were 6 years ago. Our 4th eleven entered the division 5 of the league last season and finished halfway, which is a creditable effort considering they are playing against most other clubs 2nd teams.

From my point of view, my job has become more difficult the longer I have been in the driving seat. The reasons being that having been promoted to the premier division we have found the true level at which we can play. Captaining the side during the time spent in division 2 and 1 was relatively easy as we were a far better side than the opposition teams in these leagues, so one's decisions were not so crucial and we would be on the right side of the result 8 time of of 10. Also having seen our playing strength increase, we now have a number of players in the 1st XI more qualified or who have greater experience than myself, which always leads me to think 'I hope I've made the right decision'. Thankfully a lot of the players chip in with their thoughts during the game so if I ignore their advice then on my head be it, if they were right!

During the coming season, with the pool of players we have, I believe the club should have it's most successful season ever, on and off the pitch. There is no reason, provided we all work hard, that each team cannot win the division they are in, as long as we have that little bit of luck that is always needed.

It will be quite fitting that we have to play the 1992 Somerset cup final on the County Ground, Taunton at the start of next season because of endless delays in completing the tournament this year caused by bad weather - every cloud has a silver lining!

Jeffrey Archer

Many congratulations on your centenary and I wish you every success for the future.

[signature: Jeffrey Archer]

Alembic House 93 Albert Embankment London SE1 7TY   071 735 0077

...and from Not Quite the Top

-by David Thorne
Captain Uphill Castle 'B'

Life as Captain of Uphill Castle 'B' team is a very demanding experience. At times it can be the most difficult job to undertake, at others - highly rewarding. To cope with all the ups and downs you need to be a strong and persistent character.

Probably the hardest part is selection and putting together a side for a Saturday. Once completed on a Monday night, you might think all you need to do is turn up on a Saturday morning. In an ideal world that would be the perfect scenario, but with continuous late withdrawals, you need to have a long list of replacements ready to step in at the last minute, not fair on those players you might think! Not fair on the captain either. Having to leave someone out on a Monday and then expect them to step in on a Friday night or Saturday morning is not the easiest to tasks. You try to be sincere when asking someone to play at the last minute. However, there is always a niggling doubt as to whether they believe how genuine you really are. At times this can remove all enjoyment that you get from the game and make you wonder if its all worth it.

However, once on the field, being captain gives you such a 'buzz' that the bad points are forgotten amongst the many good times during the season and it really gets the adrenalin flowing, knowing that the result of the game rests on the decisions you make - you thrive on the extra pressure. That extra pressure enables you to motivate others and produce the best of the limited resources available.

In truth, the 'B' team is not the most talented side around, but the team spirit is so good that we win games that on paper we have no right to do so. We bridge the gap in ability by fighting for 90 overs for each other, we don't play for ourselves we play as a team. Through this attitude we all put in 100% effort to ensure we win. Most people will never know how proud that makes you feel - I've had that pleasure.

From the outside many people might think they would never want the job because there's too much hassle involved. However, I must say that in the final analysis, it is a most enjoyable role to take. The experience is so enthralling that I would recommend it to anyone. It all comes down to you as an individual, have you got the determination and persistence to do it?

What does Uphill Castle 'B' stand for? Well actually it's our 4th eleven but to me B = Best.

BBC TELEVISION

FROM THE BBC WEATHER CENTRE

BRITISH BROADCASTING CORPORATION
TELEVISION CENTRE
ROOM 2050
WOOD LANE
LONDON W12 7RJ
TELEPHONE: 081-743 8000
FAX: 081-749 2864

Dear Mr. Twort,

Many Congratulations on celebrating your 100th Anniversary. May the sun always shine on your matches.

Best Wishes,

Michael Fish

Michael Fish.

Uphill from Down Under

-by Jack Rowan

The Australian connection with Uphill Castle Cricket Club now spans six seasons. During that time no less than five of us have made the pilgrimage from the antipodes to the very grass roots of cricket, the English Village Cricket Team. However I should say that prior to this I had been to England in 1977, and played for Burnham Cricket Club but went with Uphill Castle on their tour to the Sussex coast - a very dog-eared photograph bears testament to this but it was all a long time ago and much has been forgotten (although I do remember being taken shopping in Brighton for some strange "equipment").

On to 1987 and my first meeting with the boys at the club. There were so many of them. How would I remember all their names? Then a few familiar faces from that original tour: Rick Twort, Dave Harding, Dave Bickell, Chris Slocombe, Graham Board, Roy Curry and Martyn (The Bear) Mansbridge. Suddenly a car arrives in the centre of the ground, two very "wobbly" blokes complete with hats and dangling corks run over, introduce themselves as "Doc" and "Fry" then ran off and returned to the Dolphin. At that point it seemed the boys from "Down Under" were locals.

Fortunately for me the Uphill approach to cricket resembles the attitude of my other club, Stockton in New South Wales. Play the game hard on the field, play it hard off the field and luckily for me I have some willing companions on both shores.

Uphill's centenary is a real achievement. Only the committed clubs manage to reach this milestone. With Graham Board, Chairman, Gareth Williams, Club Captain and the workhorses such as "Doc" and "Fry" in control the future and growth of Uphill is certain.

Enjoy your centenary, it happens only once!

Dreadlock Holiday

The Tour
- by Ray Dibben

Before Uphill Castle was even ninety years old, 10 c.c. had a hit record featuring a line that started "I don't like cricket, I love it!" This is an edict that every member of the Castle holds dear. It is probably even more true when applied to those players who went on tour to Yorkshire last year, trading under the title "Nervous Nineties II ... The Tour".

While plans for the Centenary season were being made to tour Liverpool the Nervous Nineties tours to Yorkshire were already a regular part of the club calendar. In writing this article, I would like to report on one particular match at Hatfield on the 1992 trip.

Batting first, Uphill registered 244 for 9 off their 45 overs. This admirable total looked unlikely after six overs with just 8 runs clocked up by Messrs. Davie and Slocombe. Fortunately, after just one scoring shot off 20 balls, Mr Davie was caught at point and the innings could finally begin. Meanwhile, the diminutive Chris Slocombe was nicely into his stride. He went on to stroke seven fours and two sixes in a splendid 69 and in partnership with Ray Dibben they put on a nervous 97 for the second wicket, which was the highest partnership of the holiday.

Ninety minutes after the game began, Dibben departed in bizarre circumstances. He gloved a ball through the gully area which was nearly caught and attempted to scamper a run only to be sent back by Chris Slocombe. Dibben made his ground safely, but collided with a massive fielder en-route. Having survived three nasty moments, in as many seconds Ray was promptly given out L.B.W. The good thing about this strange decision was that young Dave Thorne was the next man in.

To the delight of the crowd, he lasted just 90 seconds, according to scorer Mansbridge, as he tickled his fourth and final delivery through to the elated wicket keeper. Non-nervous club captain Gareth Williams was next in, to replace Chris Slocombe who had just been caught and bowled. The scoreboard read 107 for 4 off 25 overs.

Hardly a crisis with Williams just in, joined by Australian Crossdale and fellow countryman Rowan yet to strap them on. However, language problems caused immediate difficulties as Crossdale decided to run out Williams for six and leave the Castle on 125 for 5 at the drinks interval.

Brett Crossdale did not let this affect him and when play resumed, he went on to play the innings of the week. He smashed 76 not out off only 60 balls, with 3 sixes and nine fours. Mike 'Dreadlock' Holyday hit a run a ball 22 and Jack Rowan a stylish 23 off just 12 balls. Roger Fry clocked up a nervous nought and Chairman Board scored 1 not out off the last ball of the innings to leave Uphill nicely set after some mid-innings wobbly bits.

A delightful Yorkshire salad tea followed, as did victory by 19 runs, with 19 balls to spare at 19 minutes past 7. With the visitors cruising to victory, it was Gareth Williams with 5 wickets and sub fielder Chris Oultram with the vital catches that swung the game Uphill's way. The spirit that won the game was in even greater evidence in the bar afterwards and following a game of two halves, some people were sick as parrots whilst others were over the moon.

At the end of the day, the boys done great and Uphill don't like cricket ...... they love it!

Seven Decades for Uphill

- by Norman Baker

It was 1939 - I was a fifteen year old schoolboy - mad keen on cricket. My father, who had taught me how to play straight in a narrow back lane said " It's time you joined a club".

He took me along to Uphill Castle where I played a few times for the seconds. The Captain was a sprightly little man called Dick Amesbury - a good captain, who was kind to me and encouraging and helpful.

Came the war - and cricket, naturally, took a back seat. After, the game resumed, and of course, I went back to this excellent club. I played in the first team with some good players. Dave Bickell's father was a good spin bowler and a hard-hitting batsman. Ron Pope and Chris Smith were local opening bowlers who took lots of wickets. I opened the batting with Gordon Porter quite often and for one season, with an amazing character from Bristol called Ron Allen.

He was short, square, and a solid opener who made a lot of runs. But what was so unusual was his attitude towards the opposition. If they got a ball past his bat, between the overs, he would summon me to the centre of the pitch, and whisper something like "How did that jammy f——g b———d of a bowler do that!? must have been the pitch". They never heard it, but he swore incessantly and I could scarcely bat for laughing.

I took a job, where I worked Saturdays, so had to leave Uphill and play over at Weston on Sundays.

But, from time to time I turned out and watched and played for them in the local evening league. They've always had some good players and what's more important, some laughs! One of the best was when we were fielding and an opposing batsman hooked a short ball to deep square leg. One of our players who shall be nameless ran to catch it. It was very windy. He tried to catch the ball with one hand and hold his wig on with the other. He succeeded in neither enterprise and fell flat on his back. Rick

Twort and the other nine of us also fell down laughing.

Today they're still a great club. They've now got the colonials in. I'm pleased to number Murray, Brett and Jacko among my friends. In fact Jacko calls me "DAD". cheeky sod!

There's been a change though. Among the humans the club now has Bears, Slugs, Hamsters, Lobsters, Monkeys, Scrotes and such masters of the English language as Mark Patch among its members. Then there's Nigel Cook who was christened Snags at Australia House in Lower Church road after a record breaking consumption of sausages, the same night some wag baked a huge cake containing a lethal quantity of chocolate laxative, causing a cessation of 99% of all activities for a week to Messrs. Doc, Cox and Fry.

I don't need a fixture list. I always know when the firsts are at home - 'Harold' Holt's voice pierces my afternoon nap as I only live 3/4 mile from the ground. What a collection!! I've played a lot of cricket with a lot of clubs, but never a better one than Uphill Castle. They enjoy it and none of the rest of you have played for the club in the 1930's, 1940's, 1950's, 1960's, 1970's, 1980's and 1990's. Beat that Jacko - you Australian Dingbat! Good luck Uphill - see you in the 2000's - if it's warm enough.

Ground Control

- Roger Fry

'Who would be a groundsman?' I often ask myself. The poor devil is on a hiding to nothing, for whatever track he produces, someone inevitably finds fault - 'It's too slow', 'There's no bounce', 'It's playing too low'. During my past nine season as Uphill Castle's groundsman these are some of the more printable comments!

Another frustration for a groundsman is, of course, our good old British weather.

Many a Friday evening I have surveyed Uphill's ground with great satisfaction, so picturesque, with the light and dark green stripes of the square emphasising a perfect cut, the wicket looks hard and fast surrounded by the greensward of the outfield. To me, a ground unsurpassed even by Lords. Then, Saturday dawns with a groundsman's nightmare realised in one four letter word, 'RAIN'.

I comfort myself with the thought that at least the square won't be damaged today. However, the rain abates and by late afternoon the sun comes out, the players eagerly get changed and the two captains decide to play. Being told in the bar that evening that the match went ahead after all I dread the prospect of going over to the ground early Sunday morning and facing the aftermath, more reminiscent of a rugby international having been played on it than the gentle game of cricket, though easier to accept of course if Uphill won!.

I would hope that in future years Uphill might be able to afford more equipment for the ground, making life much easier. Meanwhile, as many others before me, I will continue to enjoy being the groundsman, hopefully spending long, hot summer days ensuring that Uphill Castle has the finest cricket in Somerset.

The Umpire Strikes Back

1 - Derek Crocker

My time with the Castle as an umpire began in 1970 when Tony Slocombe, then captain of the second XI 'talent spotted' me officiating in a Spotters match on the Weston ground. Such was his desperation he invited me to 'come across the road' and join his team.

I stayed until the early 80's, one of my last matches being the all night game in 1985. During that most happy time there were many remarkable incidents on and off the field, some of them well remembered.

Rain and cricket do not mix and this was proven on our ground when we once played in a monsoon. The reason for not calling it off escapes me but it must have been a case of both teams being keen for points. Everyone was soaked to the skin and finding it almost impossible to move without slipping.

The one bright moment of the whole affair was when Rick Twort fielded the ball at silly mid on and attempted a run out. Not daring to risk a throw with the ground so treacherous, he ran ball in hand towards the wicket, but he tripped, fell forward and slid on all fours and crashed into the stumps.

It was just like a scene from the Horse of the Year show. Not only was his appeal denied but he received 3 penalty points for a refusal!

In common with other club members fortunate enough to have a company car I regularly drove to away matches to minimise travelling costs. It meant of course being careful not to drink more than one or two halves. After several years of chauffeuring and alcohol avoidance, I was beginning to think my acts of self denial were being taken for granted.

But no! one day the skipper suggested that I go as his passenger. This was going to be my night especially as we were playing Westlands (Yeovil) and therefore able to enjoy the facilities of their palatial social club. In the bar after the match I surveyed the long row of beer pumps, each one delivering a different brew. I selected my initial pint and mentally arranged the batting order for the remaining dozen or so. With eyes blissfully closed and the first sip passing my lips the skipper walked in, put his hand on my shoulder and said, 'Drink up Crock, we're leaving' and we went.

The 1979 tour of South Devon was a week to remember with good weather and a game of cricket every day. The most memorable for me was the game with Abbotskerswell. It was my birthday. I was 49 and in the local afterwards I felt moved to buy a celebration jug "have you a jug landlord?" I asked innocently. "Yes" was the reply, "Fill her up" I said. It seemed strange that he didn't stoop to pick it up, that was because it was so big the rim was level with the top of the bar, to the ribald amusement of the congregation he lifted the massive china vessel into full view. It looked like a small zeppelin. It would have been cheaper to buy everyone in the pub a pint, observed one wag. He was right.

The strenuous programme took its toll and by the end of the week we could only just muster a team for the final fixture. This was to be at Timberscombe on our way home. Just how exhausting the tour had been was embarrassingly obvious when our players had to be woken up when it was their turn to bat.

Best wishes on your centenary.

2 - Roy Porter

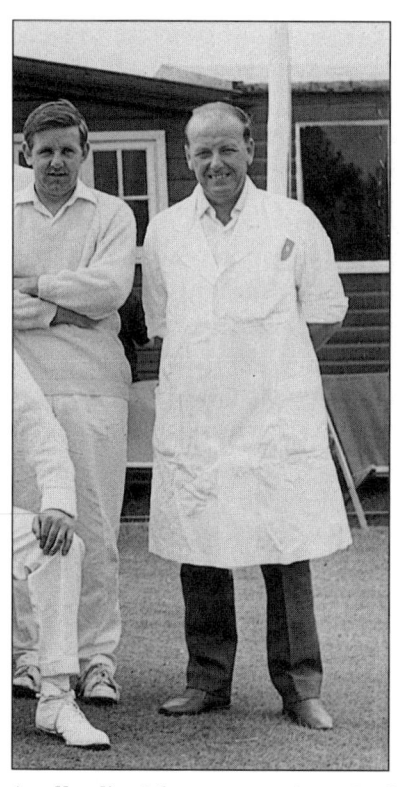

I always enjoyed umpiring both for Uphill 1st and 2nd eleven matches, and I thank all captains and players for the respect given to me.

Of course that was not always the case with opposition players. On giving a batsman out LBW he called me an unfortunate name as he passed me. However, a week later I received a letter of apology from the player himself. Obviously the Hampsett C.C. committee had instructed him to do so!!

However, in contrast I prefer the attitude of Jack Bickell in another game when I gave him out caught behind and he 'walked' without question. Jack to this day says he never touched it - a good sportsman should always act this way.

On an amusing note - once when David Reardon was bowling for Uphill at my end he had a player plumb LBW with his first ball, then his second ball bowled the new batsman with a delivery that bounced three times (ever since known as a 'three dapper') Dave was now on a hat-trick and said to me "This is it!" as he walked past and proceeded to bowl the biggest full toss that went ten feet over the batsman's head and straight into the keepers gloves. Laughter all round and Dave Reardon was more amused than anyone !

May I take this opportunity of congratulating Uphill Castle C.C. on reaching their centenary and wishing every success in the future.

3 - Ron Thorn

1993, Uphill's centenary year - how time goes by. I have many happy memories of the years as club umpire in the company of such grand players as Gordon Porter, Chris Smith, Ernie Bateman, Jack Partridge, Jack Bickell, Bob Hicks, Dickie Shaw, Charlie Bockin and many other names I am unable to recall, but real sportsmen in the true sense of the word.

I have Roy Dare, a club secretary, to thank for sending my name forward to the county club when the local clubs were asked if they had an umpire of the standard to officiate in county 2nd XI matches.

During this period I had the honour and pleasure of standing with Peter Wight (Somerset) in Ken Palmer's testimonial match at the county ground, Taunton in a match between Somerset and the International Cavaliers XI. This was the team sponsored by Rothmans and played just before the Sunday league was formed. It comprised of county players, test players (home and overseas) including a certain young Clive Lloyd who played in this match and which was televised with commentary by Frank Bough.

Two other games or rather part of, I remember were Somerset v Warwickshire in Clarence Park in 1978 between start of play until lunch as the scheduled umpire was sick and Somerset v Worcestershire at the same venue in 1987 (lunch till tea) as Dickie Bird's back was very painful at the time. I had to borrow his white coat and take the field with John Hampshire. One particular match with very happy memories was Somerset's centenary game, in 1975, played again in Clarence Park when I stood with Frank Lee. Bill Andrews and Arthur Wellard opened the bowling together for the last time - it was a wonderful sight.

May I wish the club a very happy and successful centenary year, "Head down and graft for the next centenary", you're not out yet.

Somerset County Cricket Club

All correspondence to the Chief Executive: P. W. ANDERSON

THE COUNTY GROUND · TAUNTON · SOMERSET TA1 1JT
Telephone: (0823) 272946 · Fax: (0823) 332395

Cricket Shop: (0823) 337597 · Marketing Department: (0823) 337598

1st November 1992

R. Twort,
7 South Road,
Weston-super-Mare,
Avon.
BS23 2HA

Dear Mr. Twort,

Congratulations to Uphill Castle Cricket Club on achieving their Centenary and also the part the Club has played in the promotion and well-being of cricket throughout the County during the last 100 years.

With best wishes for a successful year to all your officials, players and supporters from Somerset County Cricket Club.

Your sincerely,

R. Parsons.
CHAIRMAN

DEFINITELY A DRY BLACKTHORN DAY.

THE FUTURE

The future of the club is assured.

We now have the benefit of a long term lease agreement for the ground instead of the year to year arrangement which had operated since the club moved there 70 years ago.

There is talk of a grand scheme to replace the faithful old pavilion with facilities to rival those of Weston. It will come in time.

Meanwhile, the playing strength is clearly the strongest it's ever been and one hopes this will attract new young quality players to uphold the club's stature in future years. Indeed it may be prudent to rekindle the youth side that was so successful 40 years ago.

Never forgetting of course, the management, mentioned elsewhere in these pages who are the back-bone of the club life, handling all aspects of administration and ground work, toiling without reward other than one's quiet satisfaction that a worthwhile job is being done.

One hopes, indeed prays, that subsequent custodians of Uphill Castle will tread a similar path, but for now let's just bask in the glory of the hour ...

Club Officers

Presidents

1893 - 1918 - Major R.B. Graves-Knyfton
1919 - 1992 - Miss E. M. Graves-Knyfton
1992 -　　　Lt. Col. C.D.C. Frith OBE

Chairman
Since 1939

1939 - 1963 F.J. Cossens
1964 - 1973 W.J. Popham
1974 - 1985 J.C. Bickell
1986 - 1987 R. N. Twort
1988 - 1991 M. Baxter
1992　　　G. Board

1st XI Captains
Since 1950

1950 - C. Thomas
1951 - 1952 - E. Brown
1953 - 1955 - E. Bateman
1956 - 1957 - G. Porter
1958 - J. Partridge
1959 - 1960 - J. Sperring
1961 - J. Bickell
1962 - T. Osborne
1963 - 1968 - G. Porter
1969 - 1970 - M. Hughes
1971 - 1972 - F. O'Brien
1973 - 1977 - M. Hughes
1978 - 1980 - D. Patch
1981 - A. Slade
1982 - 1983 - G. Board
1984 - D. Patch
1985 - D. Bickell
1986 - G. Board
1987 -　　　G. Williams

UPHILL CASTLE CRICKET CLUB - PLAYING MEMBERS 1992

M. Winlow, R. Duffield, S. Tanner, M. Walker, R. Williams, S. Trego, R. Fry, A. Patel, M. Holyday, B. Crossdale,
M. Mousdale, M. Brown, D. Adams, C. Heath, P. Sloman, S. Edwards, P. Woodall, M. Baxter, J. Rowan, P. Trego, R. Parker,
D. Harding, M. Hodder, M. Patch, P. Davie, G. Board, G. Williams, R. Twort, D. Bickell, M. Mansbridge, J. Belcher, C. Oultram, M. Fisher,
M. Davie, S. Forte, T. Keight, T. Holt, C. Slocombe, N. Evans, P. Loud.

Test and County Cricket Board
Lord's Ground, London NW8 8QZ
Tel: 071-286 4405   Fax: 071-289 5619
Marketing Dept. Fax: 071-286 5583
Telex: 24462 TCCB G

Ref: ACS/JAF

30th October 1992

R Twort Esq
7 South Road
Weston Super Mare
Avon
BS23 2HA

Dear Mr Twort,

I am pleased to read that Uphill Castle Cricket Club will be celebrating its centenary next year. To reach one hundred has always been a most significant achievement in a cricketing context.

I send best wishes to the members of Uphill Castle Cricket Club and hope your next hundred years will be even more successful than the first hundred.

Yours sincerely,

ALAN C SMITH
Chief Executive

Chief Executive: Alan C. Smith   Cricket Secretary: T. M. Lamb   Administration Secretary: A. S. Brown   Marketing Manager: T. D. M. Blake   Accountant: C. A. Barker

Acknowledgments

I take this opportunity to express my thanks to the contributors mentioned in these pages. I would also like to extend my special appreciation to Mrs C.H. Savill, Mrs Pam Burnell, Mr & Mrs G. Venn, Mr C. Bagg, Mr B. Fry and Miss G. Twort for the loan of photographs; Mr Charles Howe for the photograph and his fascinating recollections; Jack Bickell, Mike Hughes and Gordon Porter for their constructive advice; Miss Claire Budd for typing my illegible scrawl, Mike Holyday for arranging the sponsors, the Weston Mercury, the Weston-super-Mare Library Staff, Dave & Gill Phelps for making the book a little more presentable, and Carole for being tolerant.

Uphill Castle Cricket Club wish to acknowledge the following sponsors, whose contributions have helped in the preparation of this book:-

Σikon Design Consultants, Nailsea
(0275) 855355

Sound Selection, Weston-super-Mare (also in Bristol)
(0934) 414476

Athlete's Foot, Sportswear Specialist, Weston-super-Mare, (also in Bridgwater)
(0934) 417945

Worlewind Videos (Branches in Worle, Weston-super-Mare, Clevedon, Nailsea and Henleaze).
(0934) 636605

P.B. Holyday & Sons, Roofing Contractors Slating & Tiling, Leadwork Specialist, Weston-super-Mare.
(0934) 627686

Weston Hire, Tool and equipment hire for home and industry, Weston-super-Mare
(0934) 632621

Carpeteria, Suppliers of carpets, rugs, vinyl & accessories (Branches in Weston-super-Mare and Burnham-on-Sea)
(0934) 627442

Uphill Motor Company, Suppliers of Vauxhall cars & vans, Weston-super-Mare
(0934) 623623

The Imperial Hotel, South Parade, Weston-super-Mare
(0934) 621275

Charlie Brown's - Sumo's 15, Carlton Street, Weston-super-Mare
(0934) 412536